WHAT NOW?

How to Live a Life of Purpose

BY

TOM KEHRES

WORD & SPIRIT
PUBLISHING

All Scripture quotations unless otherwise designated are taken from the King James Version (KJV) is public domain, and may be freely used.

What Now?
How to Live a Life of Purpose
© 2020 by Tom Kehres
ISBN: 978-1-949106-48-0

Published by Word and Spirit Publishing
P.O. Box 701403
Tulsa, Oklahoma 74170
wordandspiritpublishing.com

CONTENTS

INTRODUCTION

WE ARE MOVING into the greatest time that the Church has ever seen and God is enlisting many new soldiers into His army. They are coming by way of evangelists, teachers, preachers, and ordinary Christians who are carrying out The Great Commission;[1] people who are committed to preaching the uncompromising, life-changing, Holy Spirit-convicting Word of God, instead of the what-to-do and what-not-to-do philosophies of men.[2]

As wonderful as this end-time harvest is, so many times the new recruit is left standing alone, confused, and wondering what has happened—or what happens next. In my own experience, too many times I have seen people led to Jesus and then, after they make their commitment, they are left with no guidance or instruction on how to walk in their newfound Christianity. Traveling evangelists, preachers, and teachers will be used mightily by God in these last days, but their calling is to briefly go to a church or area and then move on. As I prayed and meditated on this situation, the Holy Spirit spoke: "Write the information down that will give the new child of God some foundation to start on.[3] This will also erase some of the old, passed-down ideas about God, and open their minds up to the Word of God and 'thus says the Lord.'"

I explained to the Holy Spirit that I had no experience or time to write such a book, but He replied that He would do the speaking and I was to do the writing. He said that if I would yield and listen to Him, He could give me a chapter in an hour that would take me three months to write. This is that book. It is not written to excuse you from reading the Word of God,[4] but I believe it will stir you up spiritually and make you hungry for the greatest love story ever written, *The Holy Bible*. If you are seeking the reality of God and a deeper relationship and fellowship with Him, this book is for you. God said "my people are destroyed for lack of knowledge."[5] I pray that this book will start you on a journey out of lack of knowledge and destruction, and into a life of victorious living in Christ Jesus.

[1] Matthew 28:18-20
[2] Colossians 2:8, 20-22
[3] Habakkuk 2:2
[4] 1 Peter 2:2
[5] Hosea 4:6

Chapter 1

WHAT AM I DOING HERE, ANYWAY?

JUST TO UNDERSTAND the reason for our very existence will clear up a lot of the confusion. Did we just "happen" here on Earth? Why are we here? Is this all there is? There must be a purpose for being here!

Genesis 1 says, "In the beginning God created the heavens and the earth." This was not the beginning of God. He always was and always will be. Yet it was the beginning of the heavens and the earth. God said, "let there be light, sky, trees, animals, the sun, and the moon." Then in verse 26, God said, "Let us make man in our image, after our likeness." You must realize that God made Earth for man, not man for Earth. God wasn't bored one week, started creating things until He finally ran out of ideas, and then decided to make a man. He made the earth, animals, trees, sky, sun, and moon with His man in mind. He created the earth as a suitable dwelling place for you and for me.[1] Without man, the earth is no good. Gold is of no value, silver of no use. The beauty of the landscape would never be appreciated. God's main creation and reason for creating everything in this Earth was man.

Why did God create us? First John 1:3 states that the reason for our existence is fellowship with each other and with our God. God made us to have a close, intimate relationship with us. God is love.[2] This is not worldly love–I love you if you love me. It is *agape* love, a giving love, whether there is a return on that love or not. For this love to be fulfilled, it must have someone to give to, someone who can receive from the lover.[3] God so loved the world, He gave. God created you to love you, and to have companionship with you forever. His desire is to be a Father with a family.[4]

This is not such a far-fetched idea when I think of the reason that I desired a child. When my boy, Joshua, came along, I didn't have him so I could be loved, or so I could rule over him, or so I could get something from him in return. I desired a child to love, to care for, to develop a relationship with, and a child to whom I could give of myself. God was no different when He had man in mind. He is not a dictator. He is not a harsh judge. He is not a slave master. He is a loving Father who desires to give to you and fellowship with you.[5] Even when we stumble, His anger lasts just a moment; His mercy endures forever.[6] You were created for fellowship with God—to become part of the family of God.[7]

---

[1] Isaiah 45:18
[2] 1 John 4:16
[3] Hebrews 11:6
[4] 2 Corinthians 6:18

[5] 1 John 3:1
[6] Psalm 103:8-11; 136:1
[7] Ephesians 2:19

Chapter 2

LOOK AT THE FINE MESS YOU'VE GOTTEN ME INTO!

GOD MADE YOU in His own image and likeness.[1] God is a spirit; therefore, you are a spirit being.[2] God created you from His own breath of life and on His own level of existence.[3] He did this so that He could have intimate companionship with you. When I went looking for someone to love and have a relationship with, I did not hunt for a dog or a cow or a cat. I needed someone on my own level of creation—a woman. God made you on His level so that He could relate and communicate with you. You are three parts—spirit, soul, and body.[4] The spirit is the real you.[5] The body that you see with your physical eyes is the tent or dwelling in which you, the spirit, live.[6] Your soul is your mind, will, and emotions. You were created to operate spirit, soul, and body, with your spirit in authority over the other two parts.

"Let them have dominion."[7] God gave man dominion and authority over Earth and everything in it. Man was to rule and reign on Earth. Adam—God's creation, God's man—was totally free and totally in fellowship with God. The only exception to his dominion was that he was ordered not to eat from the tree of good and evil, with good reason—on the day he did, he would die.[8] This gave man something that neither the angels nor any other creation had—a free will to choose. God wanted a man who was not forced to love and obey Him, but one who would *choose* to love and obey Him. Man was given a choice.

One day, the devil came into the Garden in the body of a snake and deceived Eve, Adam's wife.[9] At the same time, Adam chose, while not under deception, to eat from the tree.[10] When he did, he died instantly, as God had said—for he died spiritually.[11] (Physically he lived another 900 years. Note, spiritual death is not to cease to exist, but is separation from God.) He no longer was able to be in God's presence or freely communicate with God.[12] God was still there, Adam was still there, but the phone line had been cut.

When Adam died spiritually, he gave his God-granted authority to the devil.[13] He took on the devil's nature, becoming a child of wrath, with no hope, without God in the world.[14] This spiritual outlaw, the devil, now had authority in the earth—legal authority, because Adam gave it to him. Every person born on Earth would now be born under the authority of Satan and with his nature of selfishness.[15] God was now on the outside looking in. If He destroyed the devil, He would destroy everything linked to Satan, including His man. He could not just come in and take authority back from the devil, because the devil got it from Adam legally.

Here is an example: If I were to give you a car, and you were to give it to someone else, I would have no right to say to that other person, "Hey, give me my car back, I don't want you to have it." You had a legal right to give it away. Adam's authority was his from God, to do what he wanted with it. God's man, once created for loving companionship with Him, was now separated from Him, unable to receive from Him or communicate with Him. God is a Spirit. Man is spiritually dead. Man was now ruled by his physical senses—living by what he could see, hear, taste, touch, and smell in the physical realm only—and in helpless bondage to Satan. Or was there a way of escape?

1 Genesis 1:26
2 John 4:24
3 Genesis 2:7
4 1 Thessalonians 5:23
5 1 Corinthians 2:14; Philippians 1:22-24
6 2 Corinthians 5:1-6
7 Genesis 1:26-28
8 Genesis 2:17
9 Genesis 3
10 1 Timothy 2:14
11 Genesis 2:17; Ephesians 2:1,5; John 3:6
12 Ephesians 2:12; Genesis 3:10; Colossians 1:21
13 Luke 4:6; 2 Corinthians 4:3-4
14 Ephesians 2:1,12
15 John 8:44

Chapter 3

IN CASE OF AN EMERGENCY –
DIAL J-E-S-U-S

I WANT TO mention here, as in the Introduction, that what I am sharing with you is only a skimming of the complete love story. The only way to get the total picture is by prayer and Bible reading daily. These are not options, but a must in your walk with Jesus if you are to live in fellowship and victory.

God now saw that His man was spiritually dead. Man was hopelessly being ruled by his enemy, Satan, whose lifestyle for man is sickness, worry, fear, oppression, depression, selfishness, death, and destruction.[1] The devil took great delight in destroying God's creation and separating man from God. A redemption, or buying back, of man was needed, for Adam had sold all men into slavery.

The redemptive work had to be done by a man—a man like Adam, the one who had given away the authority. A man born of woman, living on Earth, who could pay for the sin of Adam and take back the authority from Satan. The problem was, every man was being born spiritually dead and hopelessly under Satan's rule.[2] "For God so loved the world, that he gave his only begotten Son."[3] Thus came Jesus, God in the flesh,[4] and the incarnation.[5]

As soon as God made the blood covenant—a binding agreement sealed with blood—with Abraham in the Old Testament, men of God began to prophesy of the coming Messiah. Every time Jesus' coming was spoken of by the Word of God through man's lips, that Word was in the earth and would eventually come to pass. "So shall my word be that goeth forth out of my mouth: it shall not return unto me void, but it shall accomplish that which I please."[6] The devil tried to kill every prophet who spoke out about the coming Savior, from Abel through John the Baptist, but he could not stop the birth of Jesus.

Jesus was born of a virgin named Mary, not of man, but of the Holy Ghost.[7] He was a man born with the life of God in Him, spiritually alive, like the first Adam; God in the flesh—the Son of the Living God. Yet, Jesus humbled himself, stepping down from His equality with God to become a mere man like us—not only to become a man, but to submit, obey, and die for the whole world.[8]

At the age of 30, Jesus was baptized and filled with the Holy Spirit, and the battle with Satan was on.[9] Satan attacked Him in the wilderness, in the temple, and through the mouths of men. He tried to stone Him and throw Him off a cliff, but Jesus continually used the Word of God—"It is written"—and the power of the Holy Spirit to defeat Satan at every turn. Then the time came. The price for Adam's sin had to be paid. On a cross on a hill near Jerusalem, the Son of the Living God laid down His life for you and me.

He was beaten and whipped until you could no longer tell He was even a man.[10] The crucifix on your wall does not begin to tell of the physical punishment He endured. Then He became your sin,[11] became sickness, became everything that the curse of the law entailed.[12] He cried, "My God, my God, why hast thou forsaken me?" and "It is finished." For three days and three nights He was under siege and suffered for our sins—not deserving any of it, for He was a sin-free, spotless, sacrificial lamb.[13] He did it for our sin, our failings, to get our authority back, to give our bodies healing. It was all done for us. He endured and suffered everything for us.

After three days and three nights, the price for our sin was paid in full. His death left a spotless lamb in the pit of hell, with no cause or right to be there, for He had no sin. In came the Spirit of God, the Holy Spirit, and Jesus was raised from the dead.[14] He "spoiled principalities and powers" and "made a public show of them openly, triumphing over them in it."[15] He beat Satan and beat him badly. He dragged him through hell and displayed to every demon that Satan was a whipped dog, defeated, stripped of all power and authority, leaving him beaten and powerless.[16]

Jesus was then reunited with His body, which was made immortal, and shouted, "I am he that liveth, and was dead; and behold, I am alive for evermore, Amen; and have the keys of hell and of death!"[17] All power and authority in heaven and in Earth was given to Jesus.[18] He had regained authority for man, regained victory for man, and saved the world from sin and the curse by paying your price. He suffered in hell in your place to set you free and reconcile you to God.[19] He bridged the sin gap between God and man.

The angels cried at His birth, "...on earth peace, good will toward men."[20] There is nothing separating you from God, keeping you from becoming a part of His family—nothing keeping you from fellowshipping with Him as Adam did, and becoming spiritually alive again. Jesus said, "You must be born again"[21]—born from spiritual death to spiritual life in Christ Jesus. The enemy is defeated for you.[22] He cannot stop you. All he can do is talk you out of it.[23] "...If thou shalt confess with thy mouth the Lord Jesus, and shalt believe in thine heart that God hath raised him from the dead, thou shalt be saved."[24] "For whosoever shall call upon the name of the Lord shall be saved."[25]

Do you realize that you are helpless and hopeless? Do you realize that you need a Savior? Jesus Christ, Son of the Living God, is that Savior. He's waiting for you to act. He took a terrible beating because of your sin. He went to hell and defeated every devil. He's not mad at you; He loves you. He's not holding sin against you.[26] Jesus paid the price to set you free—just so that you could say, "I'm sorry for my sin, Jesus. I hate the devil and my life and want to make a change. I want to live for You and get to know You. Come into my heart and into my life. Be my Lord and Savior. I believe You died for me, You were raised from the dead, and You now live forevermore. Jesus, come change me, and be my Lord."

Now say, "Jesus Christ is my Lord and Savior." Tell the devil, tell the angels, tell everybody that you see, that Jesus is the Lord of your life! Say it out loud, that you are a child of God and a brother or sister of Jesus. Shout it out loud, that you have been born again from spiritual death into spiritual life!

1 Deuteronomy 28:15-68
2 Romans 5:12
3 John 3:16
4 John 1:14
5 Luke 1:30-38
6 Isaiah 55:10-11
7 Luke 1:35; 1 Corinthians 15:45
8 Philippians 2:5-8
9 Luke 4:1-12
10 Isaiah 52:14
11 2 Corinthians 5:21
12 Galatians 3:13-14
13 Matthew 12:40; Acts 2:24
14 Ephesians 1:19-20
15 Colossians 2:15
16 Luke 11:21-22
17 Revelation 1:17
18 Matthew 28:18
19 2 Corinthians 5:18-20; Colossians 1:20-22
20 Luke 2:14
21 John 3:3
22 Hebrews 2:14-15
23 Revelation 12:9
24 Romans 10:9-10
25 Romans 10:13
26 Romans 5:8-10; 2 Corinthians 5:18-20

Chapter 4

WHAT IN THE WORLD HAPPENED TO YOU?

I CAN REMEMBER crying out to God in a little Catholic church in Bucyrus, Ohio, saying, "God, I am sick of my life, sick of drinking, sick of sinning, sick of being sick. If You're up there, help me. I hate my life and want to change into what You want me to be. If You're really real and can do something, help me." This was a heart cry, not a head cry. It came from deep inside my spirit, so deep that it actually hurt a little. I waited for the lightning bolt to strike me. But what struck me was a Catholic priest who simply said, "Welcome home, son, God loves you."

I was not hit with a bolt of lightning, but with a bolt of God's love. God actually loved me—ME, no-good, dirty, rotten me. His love filled my being from the top of my head into the soles of my feet. He wasn't mad at me. He didn't come to judge or condemn or punish me. He was there to love me. That night changed my life. It changed me and set me on a journey with God. It wasn't until about two years later that I actually realized what had happened to me that night. I was born, again!

In John, chapter 3, there was a man named Nicodemus, one of the chief priests of the Jews. This man "came to Jesus by night, and said unto him, 'Rabbi, we know that thou art a teacher come from God: for no man can do these miracles that thou doest, except God be with him.' Jesus answered and said unto him, 'Verily, verily, I say unto thee, except a man be born again, he cannot see the kingdom of God.'" Nicodemus was a Pharisee, a very religious man, whose life's goal was to keep all of the laws. He was exceptional in this area. He did his Sunday churches, prayed his prayers, gave his tithes, went to Sunday evening potlucks and worked Thursday night Bingo. He lectured in church and was head usher. Get the picture? But he realized that this was not enough. Something was missing. So Nicodemus came to Jesus by night. (Self-righteous people come to Jesus at night. They'll let everyone know what they are doing for the Lord, but seldom mention what the Lord has done for them. They are searching for the realization that Jesus is truly alive, and that they truly need Jesus as Lord and Savior of their lives.)

For many years I attempted to earn my way to God. I thought attending church and doing all the things that I was supposed to do was enough. Then I discovered that nothing I, my church, my works, or anything or anyone else could do would save me. Only Jesus could make me right.[1] Only Jesus could repair my relationship with God. Hold up Jesus in your lifestyle, in your conversation, in your home, in your work, and in your church.

Nicodemus said, "You teach and it has power. You speak and it makes things happen. God is all over you, and you're not even a Pharisee. I preach with little power, do no miracles, and I can't even find God. What's the secret here?" Jesus replied, "You've got a heart problem. You have to love God with your heart, not your head. But this is impossible for you to do, unless you let the Holy Spirit birth you again. You must be born again!"

You can confess sin, go to church twice a day forever, build the church, clean it, live in the church, but you must be born again. There is nothing that you can do to get good enough for God or holy enough for God to accept you. Jesus Christ, by His blood, has made you clean.[2] What can wash away my sin? Nothing but the blood of Jesus. What can make you whole again? Nothing but the blood of Jesus. Nothing means nothing. Jesus did it all. Receive it, speak it, live it, believe it. Go to church not to become, but because you *have become*. Don't serve God to be accepted, serve God because *you are* accepted. You have been reconciled to the Father through Jesus!

Your Sins Are Forgiven and Forgotten

Once you come into God's family, God has forgiven all of your sins. When God forgives, He forgets. "And their sins and iniquities will I remember no more."[3] Total remission for all our sin could only be accomplished through the shedding of blood. Faith in the sacrifice at Calvary and faith in the sin-free, spotless blood shed by Jesus has perfected forever those who are being sanctified. Every drop of blood shed at the cross was shed to wash away our sin and failures.

The only lasting sacrifice for sin is Jesus Christ.[4] If you could do enough good works to take care of your sin, then Jesus died for nothing.[5] He did not die for nothing, He died because He loved you and wanted to be a brother to you. He paid the price for all sin: past sin, "In whom we have redemption through his blood, the forgiveness of sins,"[6] present sin, "If we confess our sins, he is faithful and just to forgive us our sins, and to cleanse us from all unrighteousness,"[7] and future sin, "being now justified by his blood, we shall be saved from wrath through him."[8] He blotted them out like they never happened.[9] "I, even I, am he that blotteth out thy transgressions for mine own sake, and will not remember thy sins."[10] He took them from you and cast them into the sea of forgetfulness.[11]

If Jesus blotted them out, cast them into the sea, and forgot them, you must do the same. Forget about your past sins that happened before you were born again. Don't let Satan tie you down with, "You're so unworthy, just a dirty sinner, such a rotten person." That was all true, you were. But Jesus didn't leave you that way. He picked you up out of the pit, washed you in His blood of righteousness, and brought you home to your Father. If you sin now, run *to* Jesus, not from Him. He's your Savior, He's your Advocate, He is your Intercessor. He's faithful to forgive and cleanse. Then don't do it again. Turn from that sin and go on with God.

You Are a New Creation

"Therefore if any man be in Christ, he is a new creature." *The Amplified Bible* calls you a "new creature altogether; the old, previous moral and spiritual condition has passed away, and all has become fresh and new."[12] When you are born again, you become a brand-new spiritual being, alive spiritually, filled with the nature of God. God says, "A new heart . . . will I give you, and a new spirit will I put within you . . . I will take away the stony heart out of your flesh."[13] Although your soul, which is your mind, will, and emotions, does not change, and your body remains the same, your spirit—the real you—is recreated from the breath of God, just as Adam was created in the Garden.

You are now born of God,[14] a child of God with His nature, which is love, joy, peace, patience, gentleness, goodness, faithfulness, meekness, and temperance (self-control).[15] By developing these fruits through the Word of God and the Holy Spirit, you'll drive your previous failings of hatred, anger, selfishness, worry, and doubt out of your life.[16] Let me give you an example. If I gave you an empty glass and told you to pour the air out of it, what could you do? It's impossible. You can turn the glass upside down, but it will still have the air in it. In order to drive the air out, you must put something in, like water. When the water comes in, the air goes out. When you spend time in God's Word under the Holy Spirit's direction, you will fill up with the fruits of the Spirit and the old flesh desires will be forced out.

Many Christians today are struggling in their walk with Jesus. Sin continues to be a problem in their lives and the old flesh desires continue to rise up from within them. By spending time in God's Word, a change will occur on the inside of a person, and the result of the change will be seen in their daily conduct. God is looking to change us daily, but He works from the inside out, not the outside in.[17] Let the Word change your way of thinking and acting. We are sanctified by the truth; God's Word is that truth.[18] Romans 6 says "Knowing this, that our old man is crucified with him, that the body of sin might be destroyed, that henceforth we should not serve sin." You must come to know that you are no longer the old, ugly you. Old, ugly you was crucified with Jesus on the cross, for He took your place, was your sin substitute, and now you are able and equipped to live in victory over sin in your new life with Him. "Likewise reckon ye also yourselves to be dead indeed unto sin, but alive unto God through Jesus Christ our Lord."[19]

I often tell myself, "Oh, no, Tom, you're dead to anger and alive to patience, you're dead to selfishness and alive to love, you're dead to worry and alive to faith. You have the blood of Jesus, the Holy Spirit, the Word of God, and the name of Jesus to rule over sin." Know that you are dead to sin and alive to God. "Let not sin therefore reign in your mortal body, that ye should obey it in the lusts thereof."[20] It's your job to "let not" sin reign, not God's. Take authority over sin like you take authority over your child. Command your body how to act and your mind how to think. Tell it how to behave and don't allow it to act in any other way. This takes the Word, the Spirit, your repentance for failing, and diligence. You will not become perfect in two weeks. It took me 30 years of practice to become sinful and ugly; it will take time and a gradual growing in Christ to change. The point is you now have the power and authority to change. You are no longer in bondage to sin and the devil. "If the Son therefore shall make you free, ye shall be free indeed."[21]

[1] John 14:6; Acts 4:12
[2] Colossians 1:20;
Ephesians 2:13; Hebrews 9:22
[3] Hebrews 10:17
[4] Hebrews 10:10-14
[5] Galatians 2:21
[6] Ephesians 1:7
[7] 1 John 1:9
[8] Romans 5:9
[9] Colossians 2:14
[10] Isaiah 43:25
[11] Micah 7:19
[12] 2 Corinthians 5:17
[13] Ezekiel 36:25-31
[14] 1 John 5:1
[15] Galatians 5:22-23
[16] Psalm 119:11; 2 Peter 1:4
[17] 2 Corinthians 3:18, 4:16
[18] John 17:17
[19] Romans 6:11
[20] Romans 6:12, 14
[21] John 8:36

Chapter 5

"FREE AT LAST" – YOU SAID A MOUTHFUL

"FOR THIS PURPOSE, the Son of God was manifested, that he might destroy the works of the devil."[1] Either Jesus did, or He didn't. Either Jesus did accomplish the very reason for which the Father sent Him, or He failed. Which is it? The way you live, the way you present yourself before the rest of the world, is either a testimony of Jesus' triumphant victory or a testimony that Jesus died for nothing.

God desires for us to walk in the triumphant victory of Jesus, to no longer live in doubt and fear, speaking of our failings and weaknesses and telling others about all of our troubles and what we can't do.[2] We must no longer murmur and complain about how the enemy, Satan, is attacking our lives, our children, and our homes.[3] Some days we walk around as if Jesus is still in the grave, and Good Friday has become an everyday experience. Surely a big part of Jesus' life on Earth was His suffering and death, but I submit to you that the tomb is now empty and Jesus Christ, the anointed Savior, is alive forevermore! He sits in all authority and power at the right hand of the Father as your Advocate, your Intercessor, your High Priest, your

Representative in heaven. He is available for you, to minister to you, so that you may walk each day in His triumphant victory procession.

He "gave himself for our sins, that he might deliver us from this present evil world, according to the will of God and our Father: to whom be glory forever and ever. Amen."[4] You are free. Let me say it again—*you are free.* The only thing that can hold you back from becoming a Holy Ghost-filled, devil-stopping son of God is ignorance of who you are and what Jesus did for you. "For whatsoever is born of God overcometh the world: and this is the victory that overcometh the world, even our faith," or our believing what God says.[5] If God says you have it, you have it. What He says you are, you are. If He says that He'll do a thing, He'll do it. His Word is true, forever settled in heaven.[6] It is more sure than heaven and Earth,[7] and He continually watches over it to bring it to pass.[8]

Be careful of the *tenses* in your Christian walk. Here's what I mean: many times we spend all our time and effort to receive something or become something for God *someday.* Yet God states in His Word what you are *now, today*; what you have *now, today.*[9] And that is not by what you do, but by what Jesus did. Everything that you'll ever need—spirit, soul, and body, finances, possessions, "all things that pertain to life and godliness," here, now, and forever—are yours, bought and paid for by Jesus Christ on Calvary.[10]

"Surely he hath borne our griefs, and carried our sorrows: yet we did esteem him stricken, smitten of God, and afflicted. But he was wounded for our transgressions, he was bruised for our iniquities: the chastisement of our peace was upon him; and with his stripes we are healed."[11] If you break this Scripture down into three parts, you'll see that Jesus' death supplied you with freedom from sin and spiritual death, peace of mind for your soul, and complete healing for your physical body. Therefore, you are complete, whole, lacking nothing. It's all yours through Calvary—spiritual life, peace of mind, and divine health. You are redeemed from Satan's dominion and all of his works, rescued out of his kingdom of darkness,[12] and are now a citizen of heaven—a member of the household of God.[13] You do not need to accept or put up with anything from Satan's kingdom—worry, doubt, fear, condemnation, sin, sickness, oppression, and depression are all from the enemy.[14] "And they overcame him by the blood of the Lamb, and by the word of their testimony."[15] The precious blood of Jesus broke the power of Satan over your life once and for all.

There's Power in What You Say

Jesus Christ is now your High Priest, seated at the right hand of the Father in glory. He was anointed by God Almighty to bring all your confessions of faith to pass in your life.[16] The devil is roaming the earth looking to get you to confess your doubts, sicknesses, lack, and fears, so that these things will rule over you and come to pass also in your life.[17] Listen carefully—there is power in your mouth! Blessing and cursing come into your life through your mouth.[18] Sickness and health, lack and abundance are all a product of your words. "Whosoever shall say . . . and not doubt in his heart, but shall believe that those things which he saith shall come to pass; he shall have whatsoever he saith."[19]

What is coming out of your mouth? What do you say day-in and day-out? What are the words of your testimony? "I believe I'm catching a cold," "We're gonna go broke for sure," "I just know I'm going to get cancer because my grandfather and father had it." If you continually say it and do not doubt that you're going broke, catching a cold, or getting cancer, you can have it. If you confess "I'm blessed," "I'm healed by the stripes of Jesus," "I reign over cancer in Christ Jesus," your High Priest can bring these things into effect for you.

This is not a mental confession once in a while, but it is a result of filling up on the Word and promises of God until they run out of your heart through your mouth. "Out of the abundance of the heart the mouth speaketh."[20] What is in abundance in your heart? God's Word, or *As the World Turns?* "A good man out of the good treasure of the heart bringeth forth"—*brings forth, brings forth*—"good things."[21] Good things are what God says about you.

The Word says you're healed, you're filled, you're free, and you are living in victory. "And an evil man out of the evil treasure bringeth forth"—*brings forth, brings forth*—"evil things." What are your words bringing forth in your life? Blessings or curses? Talk sickness and you'll have plenty of it. Talk lack and you'll never have enough. The Word declares, "Death and life are in the power of the tongue: and they that love it shall eat the fruit thereof."[22] Oh, the power of that little member of your body—the tongue.[23] Use it for God's glory. Use it to praise your Creator and Savior. Use it to tell others about Jesus. Use it to become a living testimony that Jesus Christ is Lord of your life; the Savior of the world; alive forevermore.

"But I [Jesus] say unto you, that every idle word that men shall speak, they shall give account thereof in the day of judgment. For by thy words thou shalt be justified, and by thy words thou shalt be condemned."[24] Use God's words to bring your words into agreement with what He says about you, and choose life, blessing, and abundance in God's kingdom.[25] David, a man after God's own heart in the Bible, cried "Let the words of my mouth, and the meditation of my heart, be acceptable in thy sight, O Lord."[26] Claim your freedom by the blood of the Lamb, and the word of your testimony.

[1] 1 John 3:8
[2] 2 Corinthians 2:14
[3] Philippians 2:14-15
[4] Galatians 1:4-5
[5] 1 John 5:4
[6] Psalm 119:89
[7] Matthew 24:35
[8] Jeremiah 1:12
[9] Ephesians 1:3
[10] 2 Peter 1:3
[11] Isaiah 53:4-5
[12] Colossians 1:13-14
[13] Ephesians 2:19
[14] James 4:7

[15] Revelation 12:11
[16] Hebrews 3:1
[17] 1 Peter 5:8
[18] Deuteronomy 30:19; Proverbs 6:2; 12:6,18; 13:3; 15:4; 18:21
[19] Mark 11:23
[20] Matthew 12:34
[21] Matthew 12:35
[22] Proverbs 18:21
[23] James 3
[24] Matthew 12:36-37
[25] Matthew 18:18-19
[26] Psalm 19:14

Chapter 6

WARRIOR, WORD, OR WASTE

"Then said Jesus to those Jews which believed on him, 'If ye continue in my word, then are ye my disciples indeed; and ye shall know the truth, and the truth shall make you free.'"[1] "My son, attend to my words; incline thine ear unto my sayings. Let them not depart from thine eyes; keep them in the midst of thine heart. For they are life unto those that find them, and health to all their flesh. Keep thy heart with all diligence; for out of it are the issues of life."[2]

As the outpouring of God's Holy Spirit comes upon our land, and the harvest of those ready to receive the Lord is reaped all over the country, God is looking to raise up children who will grow to maturity through His Word, and become burden-bearers for the rest of His children.[3] They will become like storm shelters during a hurricane, a house on a hill during a flood, a foxhole in the midst of battle. When the trumpet blows for confrontation, the siren sounds for panic, they will not run but stand firm in the midst of hell itself.[4] They will not seek shelter, but *be* a shelter. They will not run away in fear, but toward the enemy in faith.

A thousand shall fall at their side, 10,000 cry out in terror at their right hand, but it shall not shake them for, you see, they dwell in the secret place of the Most High—not occasionally visit there, but live there, and they abide under the shadow of the Almighty.[5] They have stayed before the Lord, have attended to, heard, and acted upon God's Word. And when the storm builds and the winds blow, they do not fear, but speak boldly: "The Lord is my refuge and my fortress, my God; in him will I trust."[6] Their hearts are fixed on the Word, on the blood-bought promises of God, and they shall not be moved.[7]

When Satan comes prowling as a lion, seeking whom he may devour, he quickly moves around and avoids these warriors of God.[8] You can hear Satan and every demon of hell announce in terror, "Oh no, it's morning. He's up again and looking to destroy more of our work!" Why? Because this Christian is something special? No, because he is linked up to Jesus by the Word, and Jesus is his everything. Jesus is his strength in weakness, his light in darkness, his prince of peace in the midst of the storm. He is his shepherd in confusion, his uplifter in stumblings, his joy in sorrow, his Lord over every circumstance in his life.[9] Jesus is the solid rock of his salvation.[10]

This warrior has built his house upon the rock, for he has heard and acted upon the Word of the Most High.[11] He has built his house on the last will and testament of Jesus Christ, which was signed in Jesus' own blood on Calvary, and he knows that this Word won't fail, can't fail, unless

Jesus Himself fails. His house is strong and sturdy enough to house those others whose homes have been destroyed by the storm. You see, they built them on the sand: their own works, their own prayers, the world's ideas, man's words instead of God's words.[12] Under the warrior's roof they will find their refuge, for their eyes will be directed to the Solid Rock, the only sure foundation, Jesus Christ, the Son of God.[13]

It is not that these warriors are never under siege by the enemy, but they have become a tree planted by the river of God's Word.[14] No matter the drought, no matter the heat, no matter the recession, no matter the plagues, no matter what the world suffers, his roots go deep into the river of "thus says the Lord." His leaves will not wither, and he will always produce his fruit in due season. His branches are to shade those who are suffering the heat and the drought. His fruit is to nourish those who have fallen under the world's system. He has become Christ-like. He no longer lives, but Jesus lives His life in and through him.[15] He is always mindful of others—their needs, their troubles, their sorrows. He lays down his life for others—he demonstrates the greatest form of love.[16] The Word lives in him, so the Father and Jesus have made Their abode in him.[17] They are one.[18]

It will be your choice from this day forward whether you will desire to be the tree or live in the shade, be the fruit-producer or run around seeking the fruit of others, dwell in the secret place of the Most High or dwell in the world. The difference will be if you decide to let the Word of God dwell in you richly[19] or let the ways of the world be your life's course.[20] Jesus said, "My words are spirit, and they are life"—life to those who find them.[21] This life is borne and sustained, not by bread from the world, but "by every word that proceedeth out of the mouth of God."[22]

[1] John 8:31-32
[2] Proverbs 4:20-24
[3] Romans15:1
[4] Ephesians6:14
[5] Psalm 91
[6] Psalm 91
[7] Psalm 112:7
[8] 1 Peter 5:8
[9] Romans 10:9;
   1 Corinthians 12:3
[10] Psalm 18:2, 46
[11] Matthew 7:24-27

[12] Romans 3:20, 28
[13] 1 Corinthians 3:11
[14] Psalm 1:2-3
[15] Galatians 2:20
[16] John 15:13
[17] John 14:23
[18] 1 Corinthians 6:17
[19] Colossians 3:16
[20] James 4:4
[21] John 6:63
[22] Matthew 4:4

Chapter 7

INSIDE INFORMATION

Let me get one thing straight. To try to operate in the Kingdom of God without the Holy Spirit is to be like a surgeon who operates on a patient without making an incision.[1] Nothing will change, nothing will get fixed, there will be no healing, no recovery; you'll go through life only scratching the surface of the spirit realm when God wants to give you His entire kingdom.[2]

The Holy Spirit is your Helper.[3] He is not your doer, but the helper and the power of your doings. When you step, He'll order your steps.[4] When you open your mouth, He'll speak the Word. When you lay hands on the sick, He'll heal the sick.[5] When you begin to follow God's will, He'll bring it to pass. When you give Him an opportunity, He'll change your life and the lives of those around you! The Holy Spirit is a person, not a vapor nor a cloud, but a spiritual being just as Jesus and the Father are.[6] He is like the wind; you don't know where He comes from or where He's going, but you can see where He's been.[7] He will honor the Word of God that you speak in the same way He honored the Word of God Jesus and the Father spoke.

"In the beginning God created the heaven and the earth. And the earth was without form, and void; and darkness was upon the face of the deep. And the Spirit of God moved upon the face of the waters."[8] The Holy Spirit is ever moving, ever waiting to teach, heal, comfort, convict, and lead. "And God said, 'Let there be light,' and there was light."[9] God the Father spoke, and the Power Source of the universe, the Holy Spirit, moved and brought that word into existence. I am fully convinced that the Holy Spirit hovered over me for 30 years while I was a dead spirit in trespasses and sins, waiting patiently for me to say "Jesus, help me, be my Lord." Then He moved under the orders of my High Priest[10] and formed me into a new creation in Christ Jesus.[11]

If you want the Holy Spirit to open the Word to your understanding, to instruct you, to help you pray, to lead and comfort you, this is the key: Ask Him.[12] Yes, ask Him. Invite Him into your life. Invite Him to run your life. Don't do anything without Him, for He makes all that you do acceptable to the Father. If you are born again, He lives in you.[13] Ask the Father to immerse you in the Holy Spirit and give you His spiritual prayer language.[14] The Word tells us that the Father will not only baptize you in His Spirit, but that He also desires that you have and operate in His power. When the Holy Ghost comes upon you, you'll receive power, ability, and efficiency to witness for God.[15]

The Holy Spirit working through you will make you an able servant of God, efficient in the works of the Father and a witness to others with evidence. This is where many Christians are failing in these days. You will never be a highly effective witness without the evidence of signs and wonders.[16] No one would call you to the witness stand in today's court of law if you had no evidence to show. In these last days, there must be evidence of the supernatural power of God in the life of every child of God! We must become yielded vessels to the Holy Spirit[17] so that the gifts and power of God flow through us to free a world of people in bondage to sin and Satan.

Moses' words of, "Let my people go," were not enough to free the people of Israel from Pharaoh. It took manifestations of the power of God to break Pharaoh's hold on their lives. We must start to operate in the anointing of the Spirit of God[18] to make ourselves available to His will, so that He may move through us to others. One of the most important revelations in my own life was that the Holy Spirit wanted to do a supernatural work in my life and through my life. I begged and pleaded for Him to do it, and then I discovered that He desired to move and work through me much more than I wanted Him to! God is for us.[19] We are co-workers with God, not on opposite sides.[20] He wants to move in our meetings, in our everyday lives, and in our "prayer closets"—those places that we set aside to pray in private. He wants to mold us and shape us and set us free.

It seems that most Christians who are baptized in the Spirit have great testimonies about their very first time of "infilling" with Him "back in the day," but they do not speak about His indwelling, His presence with and in them, *now*—always here, always ready, always available. We must begin to recognize that He is in us now, this minute, and is greater than anything in this world.[21] We should start to recognize the Greater One in us instead of the trouble, worry, or trial that faces us. These will dissolve in the presence of His power and glory.[22]

My friend, you are full of the ability and power of God—full of God Himself! You are a temple of the Holy Spirit. The answer to all of your weaknesses, doubts, and fears lives on the inside of you! Begin to recognize His indwelling presence. He is in you and your ability is now limitless. God "is able to do exceeding abundantly above all that we ask or think, according to the power that worketh in us."[23] Turn Him loose! Set Him free in you. The results will be beyond anything that you can imagine or think. The results will be God's will working through your life, and freedom for a dying world. Men will run to the temple of God for healing, deliverance, guidance, and salvation. Not only that, these temples of the Holy Spirit make deliveries, seeking out the oppressed and downtrodden![24] The Holy Spirit's presence in your life will bring to pass all that Jesus purchased for you on the cross of Calvary.[25] Don't pray without Him. Don't read the Word without Him. Don't live another minute of your life without Him. "For as many as are led by the Spirit of God, they are the sons of God."[26]

1 Romans 7:18
2 Luke 12:32
3 John 14:16
4 Psalm 37:23
5 Mark 16:18
6 2 Corinthians 3:17
7 John 3:8
8 Genesis 1:1-2
9 Genesis 1:3
10 Hebrews 3:1
11 2 Corinthians 5:17
12 Matthew 7:7-8
13 1 Corinthians 6:19
14 1 Corinthians 14:2; Acts 2:4
15 Acts 1:8
16 Mark 16:20
17 2 Timothy 2:20-21
18 Isaiah 10:27; Zechariah 4:6
19 Romans 8:31
20 1 Corinthians 3:9
21 1 John 4:4
22 Romans 8:37; Psalm 91
23 Ephesians 3:20
24 Mark 16:15-20
25 1 Corinthians 2:12
26 Romans 8:14

Chapter 8

AND THE GREATEST OF THESE IS LOVE

ONE OF THE most exciting aspects of your new birth in Christ is the ability to love as God loves. The Bible says the very love of God Himself has been "shed abroad" in your heart by the Holy Ghost.[1] You were created out of the love of God. You are a love creation, created to live in love, abide in love, and be an example of God's love. "A new commandment I give unto you, that ye love one another; as I have loved you, that ye also love one another. By this shall all men know that ye are my disciples, if ye have love one to another."[2]

This love is what makes you different from the rest of humanity. Before the rebirth you were incapable of the God-kind of love, but now Love Himself lives in you.[3] People will look at you and know that there is something different about you, something special. Why? Because you'll love your enemies. You'll bless those who curse you. You'll pray for those who hate you, and you'll do good to those who mock and persecute you.[4] You will love all, not just friends and those who love you, but everyone. This God-kind of love compels you to be more concerned about other's needs than your own.[5] It causes you to deny yourself, abandon yourself, forget your interests, and seek to aid a sick world.[6] It is the kind of love that would cause God to step down and be born in the flesh;[7] to wash the feet of the disciples, including Judas, His betrayer;[8] to go to Calvary and be brutally slaughtered for all of humanity.

Jesus did not seek His own comfort, pleasure, protection . . . His own anything. He put his life aside so that others could live. Jesus Himself said, "For whosoever will save his life shall lose it; but whosoever shall lose his life for my sake and the gospel's, the same shall save it."[9] The gospel is a love story. Your life is to be a love story. We no longer love to receive love in return. We no longer love our spouse because they make us happy and fulfill our desires, but we love to fulfill their desires. We no longer love because they please us, we live and love to serve them continually, trying to please them in every way we can. There is no longer any quarrelling or harsh words, but words filled with love.

We are constantly looking, searching, for new ways to bless those around us. And when we stumble, we say, "I'm sorry, dear. If I would have been walking in love, we would never have had that argument." Love covers the multitude of sins.[10] It covers the failings of others with silence. It no longer joins in spreading the failings of others, gossiping about their weaknesses. It sees the fault, but looks at the good in the person and prays, "Father, forgive them." It sees the no-good, foul-mouthed, obnoxious man through the eyes of Jesus, as one who was important enough to die for, to be crucified for, so that he, too, could receive this kind of love.[11]

There are only two major forces in the world today—love and selfishness. Every time you speak, every time you act, every time you respond in a situation, you are either operating in one or the other—either in the I/me/my realm or the realm of love and service to others. The selfish realm will bring uneasiness, agitation, impatience, and, many times, your very own pity party. The love realm will bring joy to your heart and peace to you and others around you. It will mean that you deny yourself, pick up your cross, and follow Jesus. Your cross is to love the unlovable. Jesus died so that we may live. We, in turn, live the love life so that others may be attracted to this new life and live. Yes, it will be difficult. Yes, there will be failings at first. Yes, it will mean preferring others over ourselves.[12] It will be a carrying of the Jesus-kind of cross up the hill of Calvary and crucifying the self. But let me remind you that after the climb, after the death, comes the resurrection. You will arrive to a love plateau of perfect freedom: free to love the tax collector, free to love the prostitute, free to wash the feet of others, free to give of ourselves to others without fear. Why? Love never fails.[13]

When you walk in love, you'll never fail, because you now have known and believed the love God has had in your case.[14] You're now convinced that the love way is the only way; love words are the only words; love actions, the only actions. Love is better than arguing, better than anger, better than getting your own desires. Love never fails. Can you imagine a world full of God's love? No more angry words, no more work disputes, no more pushing in line fighting for the best seat, no more looking to move up by using others as a footstool, but a world striving to serve and meet one another's needs. If love is to win, if it is to prevail and stamp out selfishness in this world, it must begin with the Christian. It must begin with us. We have the ability.

The love-walk must be attainable or it would be unfair for Jesus to give us the command to love one another. We must begin to love each other even as Jesus loved us.[15] He didn't consider Himself, but considered the good of others. We must begin to abide in love, so that love may abide in us.[16] Yes, His Word promises when we walk in love, Love Himself will come and make His home with us.[17] Nothing will be too difficult, nothing impossible for us now, for we are walking hand-in-hand with the Master.[18] He is present, able to move in every circumstance, every trial, every situation. We must become rooted and grounded in love, drawing love from the very heart of Jesus.[19] Others will know us, not by a denomination, not by who we are, or by the position we hold, but by our love. They will not understand how they can mock us, scorn us, ridicule us, and yet we can still love them, still smile at them, still speak kindly to them. Love will win them over. Love will bring them into the fold. Love never fails.

[1] Romans 5:5
[2] John 13:34
[3] 1 Corinthians 6:19
[4] Matthew 5:44-48
[5] Philippians 2:3-4
[6] Matthew 16:24
[7] Philippians 2:5-8
[8] John 13:4-5
[9] Mark 8:35
[10] 1 Peter 4:8
[11] 2 Corinthians 5:14-16
[12] Romans 12:10
[13] 1 Corinthians 13:8
[14] 1 John 4:16
[15] Colossians 3:13
[16] 1 John 4:12
[17] Johnn 14:23
[18] Mark 9:23; Philippians 4:13
[19] Ephesians 3:17

Chapter 9

AUTHORITY IN THE NAME

"ALL POWER IS given unto me in heaven and in earth. Go ye therefore, and teach all nations. . . ."[1] Jesus' victory on Calvary was a total victory. It restored to man all that was lost in the Garden and more. The authority that Adam gave to Satan was now in the hands of Jesus Christ, the risen Lord.[2] But Jesus did not need the authority to rule as King of God's kingdom. He had all authority in heaven before he ever became a man. He took back authority to give it to us! In essence, He was saying "I got your authority back. Adam's authority over every living thing—the authority that he lost—I got back. Now you go in my authority and rule the earth."[3]

If the reborn man does not have the same authority now that Adam originally had in the Garden, then Satan's work in the Garden was more powerful than Jesus' work on Calvary. Daily talk of our weaknesses, failures, and what sinners we are is a confession that Jesus' suffering and death was not enough to break Satan's hold on mankind; not enough to restore fellowship between God and man like Adam had; not enough to allow the new creation to walk in the cool of the day in fellowship with God. Which act was more powerful—Satan's deception in the Garden

AUTHORITY IN THE NAME

or Jesus' crucifixion and resurrection? Satan's bondage or Jesus' breaking of every chain? Romans 5:17 declares "For if by one man's offense [Adam's] death reigned by one; much more they which receive abundance of grace and of the gift of righteousness shall reign in life by one, Jesus Christ."

At one time, death and sin reigned in your life.[4] But when you received the gift of righteousness, the gift of Jesus (for He is our righteousness), God's grace is much more toward you, so that you may once again reign in Christ Jesus. Much more powerful is God's grace and His gift of Jesus to you than what Adam's sin by Satan stole from man. Much more is the work of Calvary than the work in the Garden. All authority and power was reinstated to you when you were born into the family of God: authority over sickness, fear, lack, and the devil—authority to rule and reign on the earth, over every area of Satan's kingdom. "Wherefore God also hath highly exalted him, and given him a name which is above every name: That at the name of Jesus every knee should bow, of things in heaven, and things in earth and things under the earth; and that every tongue should confess that Jesus Christ is Lord, to the glory of God the Father."[5] "Neither is there salvation in any other: for there is none other name under heaven given among men, whereby we must be saved."[6]

Your authority is in that Name. The name of Jesus reigns over everything in the three worlds. That Name on your lips enables you to reign. He gave that Name among men to be used by the church. "And whatsoever ye shall ask in my name, that will I do, that the Father may be glorified in the Son. If ye shall ask any thing in my name, I will do it."[7] The word "ask" can also be translated "demand of something due." Whatever I demand of the enemy in Jesus' name, Jesus will personally see to it that it is done. What can we do in the authority of that Name? "In my name shall they cast out devils; they shall speak with new tongues; they shall take up serpents; and if they drink any deadly thing, it shall not hurt them; they shall lay hands on the sick, and they shall recover."[8] Sickness bows to that Name. Lack bows to that Name. The spirit of fear runs from that Name. There is power in the name of Jesus! All of heaven, all the angels, God and His throne are all backing that Name. When you speak in that Name, it is as if Jesus Himself were speaking.

God wants you to know, "what is the exceeding greatness of his power to us-ward who believe, according to the working of his mighty power, which he wrought in Christ, when he raised him from the dead, and set him at his own right hand in the heavenly places, far above all principality, and power, and might, and dominion, and every name that is named, not only in this world, but also in that which is to come: And hath put all things under his feet, and gave him to be the head over all things to the church, which is his body, the fullness of him that filleth all in all."[9] The name of Jesus is above every name.

Cancer is a name. Blindness, a name; depression, a name; poverty, a name; fear, a name. They all must bow to the name of Jesus. All things are under His feet. He is the head, we are the body. We are the feet! All things, principalities and demons, sickness and lack, are under us. We have allowed these things to rule our lives, to put us down—slaves, holding their masters captive! We have allowed what happened in the Garden to rule over the victory of Calvary. No longer! Our authority in that Name reigns in this life. Speak in the name of Jesus to your sickness. Speak with authority to the devil; tell him to get out of your life, your family, your finances, and don't let him back in. "And whatsoever ye do in word or deed, do all in the name of the Lord Jesus, giving thanks to God and the Father by him."[10] The name of Jesus drives out the enemy. The Name gives you an audience with the Father, any time, any place.[11] You are acceptable to God in that Name. Do all things in the name of Jesus.

I remember one afternoon as I was watching TV and my son was playing in the same room, he started to play in front of the TV, blocking my view. I said "Joshua, please move so Daddy can see." No response. So I said a little louder, "Joshua, move, so that I can see." Still no response. Then, I shouted in a loud voice, "Joshua, get out of my way!" He immediately ran into the bedroom because he knew that

I meant business. Just then the Holy Spirit said, "That's the way I want you to speak to the devil and all his works. Let him know you mean business. He's like a little disobedient child who knows when you really mean what you say."

From that day on, I speak that Name with authority. Disease has run from my family. Fear does not stay around long. They all bow and flee at the power in that Name. You have authority over your child at home, but you choose whether to exercise that authority or not.[12] If you don't, that child will run your household and do as he pleases. The same goes for the devil. You have authority over him in that name of Jesus, but you choose whether to use it or not. If not, he'll run your family and do as he pleases. If you use it in boldness, every spirit of infirmity will remember the day that Jesus mauled their master, Satan, in hell.[13] They will run in fear from that Name, as people run when a hurricane is coming to land. Dare to use that name "Jesus" and watch every knee bow and every tongue confess that Jesus Christ is Lord, and you will bring glory to your Father.

[1] Matthew 28:18-19
[2] Luke 4:6; 2 Corinthians 4:4
[3] Mark 16:16-18
[4] Romans 8:2
[5] Philippians 2:9-11
[6] Acts 4:12
[7] John 14:13-14
[8] Mark 16:16-18
[9] Ephesians 1:19-23
[10] Colossians 3:17
[11] John 16:23-24
[12] Romans 14:11
[13] Colossians 2:15

Chapter 10

PRAISING YOUR WAY INTO VICTORY

"I WILL PRAISE thee, O Lord, with my whole heart; I will shew forth all thy marvelous works. I will be glad and rejoice in thee: I will sing praise to thy name, O thou most High. When mine enemies are turned back, they shall fall and perish at thy presence."[1] We have no problem jumping and shouting when someone makes a basket, hits a home run, or crosses the goal line, but to praise the Creator of all things, to lift up our hands in worship to Him in front of others, seems to embarrass us. Praise, in your church or during your private prayer time, is a powerful tool in your spiritual walk with God, and a strong weapon against all your spiritual enemies.

Satan knows the power that's in the praise of God's people. He knows that he is helpless where praises are being offered up. He knows that he will be turned back, fall, and perish during the praise and worship of God. But worse than that, he realizes that praise will bring God on the scene. God inhabits the praises of His people.[2] Praise brings the Holy One of Israel on the scene. It is the door that God walks through and commands the storms of your life to be brought to "Peace! Be still!" When you praise, God shows up and the devil leaves. God ordained praise to silence the enemy—to stop Satan's attacks on your life and to shut him up.[3] Praise brings God; God brings deliverance. We are commanded to praise God, not for His sake, but for ours, so that He can come in power and set His people free.

King David declared "I will praise thee, O Lord."[4] Some Christians have misread this verse to say, "Yes, I feel like praising the Lord." They praise God only when they feel like it, when things are going good in their lives. It's great to praise God when you feel like it, and when things are going good. But the time you really *need* to praise God is when you don't feel like it, when your body is aching, your checkbook is on empty, your child has just colored the wall, and your dog didn't wait until he got outdoors. Then, as an act of your will, as a sacrifice of praise, cut loose with shouts of praise to your God. Your God is worthy, always worthy, to be praised.[5] No matter what the circumstance is, it doesn't change the worthiness of God to be praised. Don't praise Him *for* your trial, praise Him *in* your trial, so He may fill you with His presence and power to get you through it, to get you the victory over it.

The psalmist cried, "At midnight I will rise to give thanks unto thee . . . O Lord."[6] That's the darkest hour. When all hell is breaking loose in your life, arise and praise God. Paul and Silas were in the midnight hour. While in stocks and chains, guarded by soldiers and waiting execution, and in spite of it all, they were praising God in jail.[7] The power of praise broke their chains, opened the bars, and set them free. Feel like you're in stocks and chains? Like you're in jail, in bondage? Praising God will break you free and open the iron bars. In the Bible, King Jehoshaphat had "a great multitude" from three enemies come against his nation of Judah. As he and the people sought the Lord, the Lord gave the plan. They went into battle trusting and praising God's Word, and the king put the singers out in front of the army. He didn't put the warriors first, he put the praisers first![8]

Another leader, Joshua, looked at the city of Jericho. He saw the high, sturdy walls surrounding the city, keeping him and the people of Israel out of the city God promised to give them. What did he do? Did he say, "God's Word wasn't true? Poor us, we'll never take the city? The walls are too high, the opposition too strong?" No, he took off his shoes and worshipped. Then the Lord gave him the battle plan of praise, which was to march around the city blowing trumpets and shouting a victory cry.[9] What is the devil keeping you out of? What promise of God that belongs to you has he built a wall around to prevent you from getting it? Your health? Your finances? Your blessings? March around with the praises of God in your mouth and watch the walls fall. Then go in and possess it!

Now, a lot of people get this backwards. They want the walls to come down and *then* they'll praise God for it. They want the victory first, and they'll praise God afterwards, when they see it. But it doesn't work that way. It is the power of praise that knocks the walls down. Anybody can praise God *after* they get the victory. But it takes an act of your will, and supernatural strength, to praise God in the midnight hour. Jonah did it in the whale's belly.[10] Shadrach, Meshach, and Abednego did it in the midst of the fiery furnace.[11] Jesus did it in the pit of hell. "I will declare thy name unto my brethren: in the midst of the congregation will I praise thee."[12] When should you praise? "I will bless the Lord at all times: his praise shall continually be in my mouth."[13] Continually and at all times praise and worship the living God. In the noonday and at midnight fill your mouth with the praises of God. "Let the high praises of God be in their mouth, and a two-edged sword in their hand;"[14] to bind the principalities and powers of hell. To live in victory, let everything that has breath praise the Lord.[15]

[1] Psalm 9:1-3
[2] Psalm 22:3
[3] Psalm 8:2
[4] Psalm 108:3
[5] Psalm 18:3
[6] Psalm 119:62
[7] Acts 16:25
[8] 2 Chronicles 20
[9] Joshua 5:13-6:5
[10] Jonah 2
[11] Daniel 3
[12] Psalm 22:22
[13] Psalm 34:1
[14] Psalm 149:6
[15] Psalm 150:6

Chapter 11

FANNING THE FLAMES

SO MANY TIMES the new Christian, when touched by God, is ignited with a deep desire and a fire in his heart for God and spiritual things. He is on the mountaintop with his new life and his power in the Holy Spirit. He feels the presence of God very near to him, and the joy of the Lord fills his very being. After a short time, however, the sensation seems to ooze away, and the child of God starts to wonder if anything actually happened at all. He starts to feel dry and distant from God. Suddenly, prayer and Scripture reading, which were easy and desirable before, become hard tasks and seem to be doing little good.

When this occurred in my life, I went into a panic. I thought God had left me. The devil told me that I had sinned, that I had made God mad at me; that God took a deeper look at me and decided that I wasn't good enough to deal with or be around. I felt empty instead of full, forgotten instead of loved, dirty instead of clean. The great deceiver had come and was doing what he does best—lying and deceiving me into thinking that God didn't care about me anymore. Well, I couldn't feel God's presence anymore . . . I couldn't sense His love any longer. Where did God go and why did He leave me?

I sought help from other Charismatic leaders who simply said, "Oh, everybody goes through that at times in their spiritual walk," but I didn't like that answer. I searched and asked and read books to see where I had failed. One day during my prayer time I cried out, "God, please, come back. I'm sorry for whatever I did. Please don't leave me. Love me again. Make me clean and hear my cry." Suddenly, I heard a voice inside of me. It said, "Tom, are you calling me a liar?" I quickly responded, "No, God, never!" The voice continued, "I already promised you in my Word that I would never leave you nor forsake you until the end of time[1] . . . that nothing could ever separate you from my love[2] . . . that my Son Jesus' blood has made you white as snow[3] . . . and that my eyes are always on you and my ears are open to your cries.[4] Is my Word good? Is my Word true or not?" Yes, God's Word is true. It had become time for me to start to walk by faith in God's Word and not by my sight or feelings.[5]

Every morning I would go to my prayer room and say, "I may not feel like You are here, but I know You are, God, because You told me in Your Word that You would be. It may not seem like my prayers are doing anything, but I know that You hear me and if I ask, I will receive." Shortly after that, the feelings that I once had, the fire and the tangible presence of God that once had been there, followed these professions of faith in my life, and I have seldom gone a day without them since. You see, I was trying to *feel* something in order to believe, instead of believing God—and *then* experiencing the feeling. Feelings should not proceed—*come before*—faith. You do not believe because you feel—you believe because God said so . . . and *then* you will feel His presence. To grow up in God, we must continually look at the things that are unseen instead of the things that are seen.[6] We must look at the Word and not our surroundings.

On Fire!

I would like to share with you four things that will keep you "on fire" for God. If you continually practice these things in your daily life, you'll become a revival in yourself that will spill out into others' lives!

Forget not all God's benefits. Psalm 103 says, "Bless the Lord, O my soul: and all that is within me, bless his holy name. Bless the Lord, O my soul, and forget not all his benefits." Never forget what God in His mercy and grace has done and is doing for you: How He changed your course, your destiny. Sent His Son in love. Filled you with His Spirit. Protects you every day from evil. Made you His child. Find the millions of blessings of God in the Word and mark them.

Daily thank and praise Him for what He has done and for His love and grace. Forget not His many benefits.

Intercede for others. Spend time daily "standing in the gap" for others, for the lost, sick, and lonely, for other Christians. Pray for people and their needs, and the love of God "shed abroad" in your heart by the Holy Ghost will start to flow out of you. Get "you" off your mind and concentrate on others, and God will take care of you. Use your prayer language in the Holy Ghost to pray for those whom God puts on your heart. The Holy Spirit knows what and how to pray when we don't. God told me once that many people will see hell because the Body of Christ has neglected to pray, neglected to lay down their lives for others. We've gone to sleep and watched as prayer was removed from our schools and abortion became rampant in our land. The time is now to return to our knees so that God can move once again in His nation.

Read and repeat God's Word. The word "hearken" in the Bible means to "hear it and speak it." When I discovered this several years ago, I would walk around the house proclaiming the Word of God to myself. I would say out loud who I was in Christ Jesus, who God was, who Jesus was, and what He had done for me, as well as what He was doing at that moment for me at the right hand of the Father.[7] I would thank God that I was healed from the top of my head to the soles of my feet,[8] that my needs were met,[9] that I was a child of God,[10] a joint-heir with Jesus,[11] that I was filled with the Holy Spirit,[12] and was more than a conqueror.[13] Before long, these Bible truths became real to me. Confession of the Word with thanksgiving brings possession.[14] These words will go from a mental reminder to a powerhouse of faith in your spirit. You'll get to the point that no one can tell you any differently—nobody—no demon, no doctor, no naysayer. These Scriptures will change from being nice promises to becoming your possessions, and you will begin to walk in them. Through the Word and the Holy Spirit, you will begin to realize you actually are what they say you are.

Evangelize others—tell them the good news of Jesus. God states that His will is that all men become saved and come into the knowledge of the truth.[15] God will do the saving, but you must speak the truth.[16] Share Jesus with others. Become a light to this dark world. Be the salt of a world that has lost its flavor.[17] Confess Jesus before others and He will confess you before the Father.[18] You are anointed and appointed as an ambassador of God to share the Word of reconciliation.[19] Go into all the world and preach the Good News.

These four things will keep you hot for God and make your Christian life an exciting adventure with Him. The key word is *"daily." F*orget not, *I*ntercede for others, *R*ead and repeat the Word, and *E*vangelize. These are all daily commitments for a daily walk with God, and a full life of amazing, God-glorifying victory.[20]

[2] Romans 8:39
[3] Isaiah 1:18
[4] 1 Peter 3:12
[5] 2 Corinthians 5:7
[6] 2 Corinthians 4:18
[7] Hebrews 7:25
[8] 1 Peter 2:24
[9] Philippians 4:19
[10] Galatians 3:26
[11] Romans 8:17
[12] John 14:16
[13] Romans 8:37
[14] Hebrews 11:13-16
[15] 1 Timothy 2:4
[16] Romans 10:14
[17] Matthew 5:13-15
[18] Matthew 10:32
[19] 1 John 2:20; 2 Corinthians 5:19-20
[20] John 10:10; Hebrews 13:20-21

ABOUT THE AUTHOR

TOM KEHRES is senior pastor at Treasure Coast Victory Center in Fort Pierce, Florida. He is married to his wife, Becky, and has two sons, Joshua and Aaron, and two daughters-in-law, Amber and Brandi. He founded TCVC in the year 2000 and also formed the Treasure Coast Training Center. He has hosted the local TBN television show several times and also has been a guest on the show. His heart is to grow up the body of Christ through knowledge of the Kingdom of God and through the revelation of "Christ in you."

To contact Tom go to
E-mail : bubbleup7777@aol.com

Treasure Coast Victory Center
3212 South U.S. Highway 1
Fort Pierce, Florida 34982